Good Queen Bess

The Story of Elizabeth I of England

By Diane Stanley and Peter Vennema
Illustrated by Diane Stanley

HarperCollins *Publishers*

TO
BESS
AMELIA

WELCOME TO THE WORLD

The authors wish to thank
Dr. Amos C. Miller,
professor of history at the University of Houston,
for his critical reading of this book.

The text of this book is set in 13-point Weiss.
The illustrations are rendered in gouache.

Good Queen Bess
Text copyright © 1990 by Diane Stanley Vennema and Peter Vennema
Illustrations copyright © 1990 by Diane Stanley Vennema
Printed in the U.S.A. All rights reserved.
First published in 1990 by Four Winds Press.
Reissued in hardcover by HarperCollins*Publishers* in 2001.
Published by arrangement with the authors.
www.harperchildrens.com
Library of Congress Cataloging-in-Publication Data
Stanley, Diane.
Good Queen Bess : the story of Elizabeth I of England /
by Diane Stanley and Peter Vennema ; illustrated by Diane Stanley.
p.   cm.
Originally published: New York : Four Winds Press, c1990.
Includes bibliographical references.
ISBN 0-688-17961-4 — ISBN 0-06-029618-6 (lib. bdg.)
1. Elizabeth I, Queen of England, 1533–1603—Juvenile literature.
2. Great Britain—History—Elizabeth, 1558–1603—Juvenile literature.
3. Queens—Great Britain—Biography—Juvenile literature.
[1. Elizabeth I, Queen of England, 1533–1603.   2. Kings, queens, rulers, etc.
3. Women—Biography.]   I. Vennema, Peter.   II. Title.
DA355.S73   2001   942.05'5'092—dc21   [B]   00-047267   CIP   AC
1   2   3   4   5   6   7   8   9   10

AUTHOR'S NOTE

Nearly twenty years before Elizabeth I was born, a religious movement began that divided the Christians of western Europe into two opposing groups, Catholics and Protestants. This movement was known as the Reformation.

The Protestants (or "protesters") left the Catholic Church because they felt it had become too powerful and that some of the priests were more interested in money than in religion. The Protestants opposed some of the Church's beliefs and practices, and they rejected the Pope as head of the Church, preferring to choose their own religious leaders.

In those days, religion was not a matter for people to decide for themselves. Each country in Europe had a state religion that was enforced by law. Throughout Europe a dreadful tug-of-war was taking place between Catholics and Protestants, bringing with it riots, burnings, and death. As this story will tell, Elizabeth acted with tolerance and moderation in religious matters, and spared her country much of the horror of these troubled times.

ING HENRY VIII OF ENGLAND WANTED A SON. HE had been married for seventeen years, and in all that time only a daughter, Mary, had survived. As each year passed, he grew more desperate.

He knew he could not live forever. Someday one of his children would rule England, and that child was supposed to be a boy. A woman on the throne would mean trouble, for she would have to marry to produce an heir. Marriage to a foreign prince would put England under the power of the husband's country. Marriage to an English nobleman would give power to the new king and his friends, dividing the English people into warring factions. Besides, Henry did not believe that women were wise or strong enough to rule a country.

He made up his mind to end his marriage to Catherine of Aragon and find a new wife—someone young who could have lots of children. But Henry was a Catholic, and divorce was not allowed by the Church. So the king sent messengers to the Pope, the spiritual leader of all Roman Catholics. He asked the Pope to declare that the marriage had never really been legal in the first place. But no matter how often Henry asked, the Pope always refused. So in 1533 Henry formed the Church of England and made himself the head of it. This meant that men and women throughout England were forced – no matter what their true beliefs might be – to join the new Church of England.

The new Church supported his views on the marriage question, and the king soon had a new queen, Anne Boleyn. And the queen had news: she was expecting a child!

As the time came close for Queen Anne to give birth to the new heir, Henry asked the physicians and astrologers: would it be a boy or a girl? They all agreed it would be a boy.

On September 7, 1533, the child was born. It was a girl, and they named her Elizabeth.

Now Anne, too, seemed unable to produce another living child. Three times she became pregnant, only to lose the baby. Henry grew reckless. Before Princess Elizabeth was three, Queen Anne had been put to death for treason, and Henry had married a third time. His new wife, Jane Seymour, finally gave him a son, Edward. At last the future of England was secure.

After Jane's death, Henry went on to marry three more times, though he would have no other children.

Elizabeth was no longer so important now that England had a prince. She did not live at court with her father, but grew up at the Palace of Hatfield, where she had her own governess, servants, and teachers.

Though Henry didn't think his daughters were fit to rule England, he did believe in giving them a good education. Elizabeth's teachers were great university scholars. And she was an intelligent and hardworking student, with a marvelous memory.

In the morning she studied Greek, and in the afternoon she studied Latin. Elizabeth had such a gift for languages that she learned Italian, French, and Spanish, too. She was also talented in music, and her handwriting was admired for its beauty.

When Elizabeth was thirteen, Henry died, and little Edward—who was only nine—became King Edward VI.

Elizabeth continued to live quietly under her brother's rule, but as she grew into a young woman she came to realize that being a princess could be dangerous. There were many ambitious men in England who were always looking for ways to gain power. A few even hoped to be king and thought up plots to marry Elizabeth and take the kingdom in her name. That, of course, was treason, and the punishment for treason was death. Elizabeth learned very early to choose her friends carefully, not to put things in writing, and to beware of what she said.

Edward—the son Henry had risked so much to have—was never strong or healthy. He died six years after becoming king. And just as Henry had feared, there was a scramble for the throne. One of those ambitious men had married his son to Lady Jane Grey, a member of the royal family, and had influenced the dying Edward to name her heir to the throne. Lady Jane was only queen for nine days before she was imprisoned in the Tower of London.

Now Princess Mary, Elizabeth's half sister, became queen. To the horror of the English people, she decided to marry Prince Philip, the future king of Spain. The people believed that Philip didn't care about England and only wanted to use it to help his own country. They worried that he would drag little England into Spain's wars, and that he might even take away the rights guaranteed to Englishmen in the Magna Carta. And since both Mary and Philip were devout Catholics, the people of England (who had finally accepted the new Protestant Church of England) were forced to change their religion all over again. A mood of rebellion swept over the countryside.

A plot soon formed to get rid of Mary and make Elizabeth queen instead. But it failed, and the young princess was taken to the Tower. Her own mother had gone to her death from there. So had Lady Jane Grey, the innocent victim of that other failed plot. Would the same thing happen to Elizabeth?

For two months, she waited in fear. Finally, since Mary could not prove anything against her sister, Elizabeth was sent away to a distant and decrepit palace (only four rooms were fit to live in), where she was kept under house arrest.

The mood in England grew darker. When some of Mary's subjects clung to their Protestant faith, she burned almost three hundred of them for heresy. The people gave her a bitter nickname: "Bloody Mary."

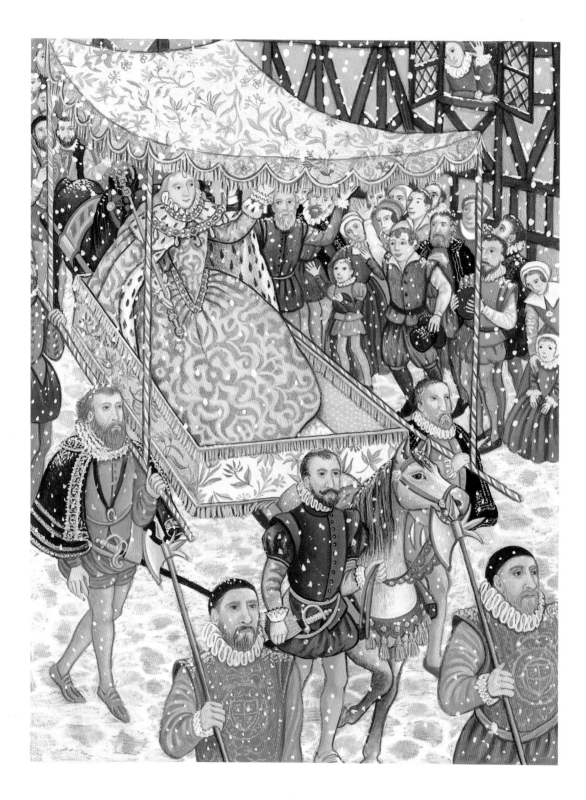

On November 17, 1558, after ruling only five years, Mary died, leaving no children. To the delirious joy of the people of England, Elizabeth became queen. She was twenty-five years old.

After the banquets and dances were over, Elizabeth set to work. One of the first things she did was choose her chief advisor, Sir William Cecil. Elizabeth was a good judge of men, and Cecil was honest, wise, and faithful. He thought she was the "wisest woman that ever was, for she understood...all the princes of her time and was so perfect in the knowledge of her own realm, that no councillor she had could tell her anything she did not know before." Cecil would serve her as Principal Secretary for forty years, and when he died at the age of seventy-eight, his son Robert would carry on in his place.

Elizabeth planned to return to the Protestant Church of England, but she was very tolerant. So long as people attended church now and then, she didn't really care what they believed. She said she didn't want to "make windows into men's souls."

Elizabeth knew that France and Spain, both powerful Catholic countries, were a real threat to England. She must somehow keep them from uniting against her, for her army was weak and the royal treasury nearly bankrupt. But this challenge suited Elizabeth perfectly, for it was her style to use her wits rather than force. She knew how much she could gain by stalling, changing her mind, and playing one side against the other. It helped that she did her dealing with foreign ambassadors herself, as she spoke their languages. Through clever and subtle manipulation, she managed to keep England out of war for twenty-seven years.

Elizabeth used these tactics not only with foreign countries, but also with her own councillors. She rarely met with them as a group, since they might unite to overwhelm her. She talked with them separately and sometimes played on their feelings of rivalry to divide them. She didn't mind throwing a temper tantrum now and again if that would gain time, change the subject, or win her point. Once she had heard the opinions of her advisors, she made her own decisions, and she expected to be obeyed.

Everyone expected her to marry, so that she could have children to rule after her. Some thought she needed a husband to "relieve her of those labors which are only fit for men." (That was what her former brother-in-law, now Philip II of Spain, said when he offered to marry her.)

Elizabeth was far too wise to marry Philip, who had already brought England so much grief. But how about Prince Eric of Sweden, who wrote her passionate love letters in Latin? Or Ivan the Terrible of Russia? Either Archduke Ferdinand of Austria, or his brother Charles? She didn't say no, she didn't say yes, she said maybe. She went on being vague and inventing difficulties and changing her mind and taking up time. If others hoped to marry her to gain England, she would pretend to consider marriage to gain what *she* wanted—time, alliances, and influence with other countries. And besides, as long as she was single, no one could tell her how to run her country.

If she could have married for love—as no queen could—she would have chosen Robert Dudley, Earl of Leicester. But he was not important enough to marry a queen, and besides, he already had a wife. Still, Leicester was her lifelong good friend, and he loved and served her for thirty years.

When Elizabeth was twenty-nine, and still not married, she fell dangerously ill with smallpox. Her councillors were horrified. If they lost their young queen now, without a clear successor, anyone related to the royal family might claim the throne. And that could mean civil war.

She recovered, but her councillors were badly shaken. They begged her to marry and give England an heir to the throne. If she wouldn't do that (and it began to look that way), then she must choose her successor. But she knew how plots grew up around the heir to the throne, so she wouldn't do that, either. When it came to a clash of wills, the two houses of Parliament and all her councillors combined were no match for Elizabeth.

For all of Elizabeth's life, men would make the mistake of thinking she was "only a woman." But Elizabeth turned what should have been a weakness into an asset. Because she was a beautiful young queen, and an unmarried queen at that, all her court—and all the country—were half in love with her.

Her court was a lively one, with everyone striving to outdo one another with elaborate clothes and jewels. The men even dyed their beards purple or orange to match their coats. There were tournaments, festivals, and dances, and Elizabeth always came to them gorgeously dressed, making a point of showing herself among her people. No wonder a foreign visitor at court wrote home, "It was more to have seen Elizabeth than to have seen England!"

Every month or so, the court packed up and moved so that the palace could be scrubbed from top to bottom, for this was in the days before sanitary plumbing. This was also the time when the dreaded disease called the plague stalked the country. Whenever there was an outbreak nearby, the queen and all her court hurried away.

But Elizabeth did not just go from palace to palace as the English nobility had always done before. Every summer she and her entire court went "on progress," visiting the great manor houses of important noblemen throughout the country.

Hundreds of carts heaped with luggage, furniture, and supplies followed the procession as it rattled along over rough roads. Every stop had to be planned ahead of time, so that food could be cooked and waiting when Elizabeth's party arrived, and so that everyone would have a place to stay at night.

When the queen arrived at each nobleman's house, she would be entertained with banquets, plays, music, and lavish spectacles, such as mock sea battles or fireworks. Her host was also expected to give her rare and expensive gifts. The cost of such a visit could be staggering.

But there was more to all this traveling about than a change of scene. Elizabeth was learning about the different parts of her country and meeting her subjects. She usually rode openly on horseback so that everyone could see her. She stopped in little villages and listened graciously to long speeches, received humble gifts of cakes or flowers, gave her hand to be kissed, and won the hearts of her people. They called her Good Queen Bess.

To the north, in Scotland, things were not so peaceful. The Scottish queen, Mary, was suspected of plotting the murder of her husband. To make matters worse, she then married the suspected murderer. She was imprisoned and forced to give up her throne to her baby son, James.

Mary was Elizabeth's cousin, and when she escaped from her prison and crossed the border into England, she asked for her cousin's protection. What could Elizabeth do?

She couldn't send her back to Scotland, for it would probably mean Mary's death.

To let her go abroad to France or Spain would be too dangerous. Mary was a Catholic, and she had a good claim to the throne of England. The Catholic nations of Europe would be tempted to send an army to England to make Mary queen.

Obviously, Mary must remain in England. The English held a tribunal to look into the charges that she had conspired to murder her husband, and concluded that she was probably guilty. She was confined in Sheffield Castle, and although she kept her servants and her queenly way of life, she was not free to leave. Mary would spend the rest of her life being shuttled from one royal prison to another and doing everything in her power to win her freedom.

Mary had not been imprisoned long when she told a servant of the Spanish ambassador, "Tell the ambassador that if his master [King Philip II of Spain] will help me, I shall be Queen of England in three months, and Mass shall be said all over the country."

Within six months, powerful Catholic lords in the north of England revolted, and Elizabeth had to send an army to stop them.

Elizabeth suspected Mary of communicating secretly with England's enemies, but Mary claimed to be innocent. She wrote Elizabeth sweet letters begging for a chance to meet face-to-face. She sent gifts, including needlework she had done herself. Elizabeth answered her cousin warmly, but each time found excuses for not meeting. The strange relationship between Elizabeth and Mary would drag on in this way for twenty years.

When Elizabeth was entering middle age she began another marriage negotiation, this time with France, to marry the king's younger brother. This boy, Francis, Duke of Alencon, was less than half her age. Not only that, but he was under five feet tall, with a huge nose and a face deeply pitted by small-pox. This worried Elizabeth, but if she was ever to have children—and give England an heir to the throne—she must do it now. At forty-six her time was running out.

Alençon came to England secretly, in disguise. Although he was just as ugly as Elizabeth had been told he was, she liked him immediately, for he was civilized and intelligent and spoke cleverly. She called him her "Frog," and delighted in their hours together. It looked as though, at long last, England would have a king.

Now it was Elizabeth's councillors and her people who were against her marriage. Books protesting the French marriage appeared mysteriously in her room. Ministers spoke against it from the pulpit. It was all a matter of politics and religion, but then, that's all a queen's marriage was about. Her sister Mary had ignored the wishes of her subjects when she had married Philip. But Elizabeth was wiser. She knew she would have to give in. The only marriage she would ever have would be to her kingdom.

Elizabeth had little time to bemoan her disappointment, for England was entering a dangerous period. Fairly early in her reign, Pope Pius V had published a statement that Elizabeth was no longer a part of the Catholic Church, and since she was a "heretic queen," her Catholic subjects no longer had to obey her. From that time on, the Pope, Spain, and many Catholics worked together to overthrow Elizabeth and return England to Catholic rule.

As these efforts became ever more intense, Elizabeth's councillors and the members of Parliament grew afraid for her life, and in 1581 they passed strong anti-Catholic laws. Though Elizabeth hated such laws, she knew that her powerful Catholic enemies not only put her life in danger but put the peace of England at risk. All she could do was see that the laws were not carried out too strictly. She would not repeat the horrors of "Bloody Mary's" reign in hers.

But there was one Catholic whom her councillors and Parliament feared and hated most: Mary, Queen of Scots. They called her "a monstrous and huge dragon," and they demanded her death. Elizabeth refused. The thought of executing a queen—her own cousin—was horrible to her, no matter how guilty she might be.

At this time, Elizabeth had a second Principal Secretary, Francis Walsingham, who was determined to find proof of Mary's guilt that even Elizabeth could not overlook. He set up a scheme to learn the contents of Mary's secret letters.

This is how it worked. When letters came from France or Spain, they were given to a young man named Gilbert Gifford, one of Mary's spies. Alas for Mary! Her spy had been caught and had become England's spy. Now he betrayed her. Gifford gave the letters to Walsingham, who copied them and had the code deciphered.

He then gave them back to Gifford, who took them to a certain brewer who supplied Mary's beer. This man wrapped the letters in a watertight case and slipped them into a beer barrel, which was delivered to the castle. Mary thought she had cleverly outwitted everybody with her beer barrel trick, and she fell right into the trap. She wrote dangerous answers, and these took the same path on the return journey.

Walsingham's net caught many fish. A group of young men were conspiring against Elizabeth, and they wrote to Mary about it. She approved of the plot in writing; she even offered advice. There were also letters from Spain showing that Philip was preparing an armada, a great fleet of ships, to help in "the setting of your Majesty at liberty."

Fourteen conspirators were executed; Mary was tried and convicted of treason. For months, Elizabeth, who hated bloodshed, would not sign the death warrant. But at last, on the morning of February 18, 1587, after twenty years in prison, Mary died bravely. She and Elizabeth, whose lives were so tied together, had never met.

The people rejoiced, Elizabeth mourned, and France and Scotland fumed. And in Spain, Philip pledged to undertake a holy crusade against this heretical queen.

When the Spanish Armada sailed, church bells rang throughout Spain. In his private chapel, Philip knelt for hours, praying for a victory.

In England, the army camped on the coast at Tilbury, expecting the Spanish to land any minute. The soldiers grew wild with joy and devotion when they saw their queen riding through the ranks in steel armor, "like some Amazonian Empress."

"Let tyrants fear!" she cried to the crowd. She had come, she said, "in the midst and heat of the battle to live or die amongst you all...I know I have but the body of a weak and feeble woman, but I have the heart...of a king—and a king of England, too—and think it foul scorn that...any prince of Europe should dare to invade the borders of my realm." Could any king in Europe match this queen?

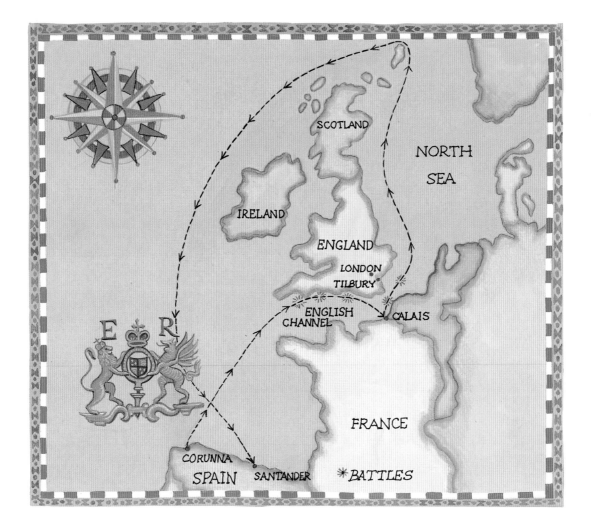

On July 29, 1588, the armada was sighted off the coast of England. Elizabeth and her army waited as the English and Spanish ships did battle. Spain had long been the greatest sea power, but England's ships were newer and of a more modern design, for Henry VIII had begun building the navy only a generation before. These ships also had long-range guns mounted on the sides, which the Spanish ships did not have, and better-trained captains and seamen to sail them.

The battle was going poorly for the Spanish, so the armada retreated to Calais on the coast of France, where the ships dropped anchor. But the English set a number of boats ablaze and sent them into the midst of the Spanish fleet. In terror, the Spanish ships scattered—and the English were waiting for them. Only a terrible storm saved Spain from certain defeat. Just over half the armada returned to Spain, while not a single English ship was taken.

Throughout Europe the defeat of the armada was said to be the will of God. It brought England a time of peace and security and the full flowering of the Age of Elizabeth. Her court had become a great cultural center, where men of genius found the friendship and financial support they needed to make their place in history.

The greatest artists of the day came to Elizabeth's court to paint portraits of her noblemen and ladies. Famous musicians came there as well, and poets wrote poems praising the queen.

There were great Elizabethan adventurers, too, such as Sir Francis Drake, who was the first Englishman to sail around the globe, and Sir Walter Raleigh, who founded the colony of Virginia in the New World.

But it was the theater that was the crowning glory of Elizabeth's age of culture. Because the queen and her friends loved drama, new theaters were built and playwrights were encouraged to write plays for them. There were some people in England who wanted to close the theaters—they thought they were sinful—but Elizabeth wouldn't allow it. Had it not been for her, we might never have known the work of William Shakespeare, who wrote the greatest series of plays in all history.

Elizabeth deserved to be proud of her accomplishments. But she was the last of the Tudor line, and she was growing old. One by one the great men and women of the age were passing away. Mary, of course, was gone. Then Elizabeth lost her beloved Leicester, then Drake. Cecil and Walsingham died. Even her archenemy Philip II was gone. She had outlived them all.

But the loss that may have grieved her most was that of the dashing Robert Devereux, Earl of Essex. He had been her great favorite in her old age. Yet tragically, he grew too ambitious and tried to raise a rebellion against the queen. It was her grim duty to sign his death warrant for high treason.

When she addressed Parliament in November of 1601, everyone suspected it might be for the last time. Nearing seventy, she was thin and frail. She wore a red wig "of a color nature never made" over her thinning hair. White powder and bright rouge gave her face a startling appearance. What she said that day has gone down in history as Queen Elizabeth's Golden Speech. She spoke from her heart: "Though you have had—and may have—many mightier and wiser princes sitting in this seat, yet you never had—nor shall have—any that will love you better."

She had lived to a greater age than any English ruler before her, but in her seventieth year, her health broke.

Elizabeth had never named her successor, yet the choice was clear to everyone: Mary's son, James VI of Scotland. He was ready to ride to England as soon as he heard the queen was dead.

He did not have to wait long. In the early morning of March 24, 1603, in the 45th year of her reign, Queen Elizabeth died peacefully in her sleep.

All Europe stopped to pay homage to this great queen. Even her enemies admired her. Pope Sixtus had written, "She certainly is a great queen ... just look how well she governs! She is only a woman, only mistress of half an island, and yet she makes herself feared by Spain, by France, by the Empire, by all!"

It would not be Henry VIII or Philip II or any of the kings of France who would give their name to the age they lived in. It would be called the Elizabethan Age after the remarkable queen who loved her people so dearly and ruled them so well.

BIBLIOGRAPHY

Erickson, Carolly. *The First Elizabeth.* New York: Summit Books, 1983.

Jenkins, Elizabeth. *Elizabeth the Great.* New York: Coward-McCann, 1959.

Neele, J. E. *Queen Elizabeth I.* London: Jonathan Cape, 1934.

Orlandi, Enzo, general editor. *The Life & Times of Elizabeth.* Philadelphia: Curtis Publishing Co., 1967.

Ridley, Jasper. *Elizabeth I, The Shrewdness of Virtue.* New York: Viking Penguin, 1988.

Smith, Lacey Baldwin. *The Horizon Book of the Elizabethan World.* New York: American Heritage Publishing Co., 1967.

Strong, Roy. *Gloriana, The Portraits of Queen Elizabeth I.* London: Thames and Hudson, 1987.

Williams, Neville. *All the Queen's Men, Elizabeth I and Her Courtiers.* New York: Macmillan Publishing Co., 1972.

————. *The Life and Times of Elizabeth I.* Garden City, N.Y.: Doubleday & Co., 1972.

Young readers who wish to find out more about Elizabeth might enjoy reading the following books:

Bush, Catherine. *Elizabeth I.* New York: Chelsea House Publishers, 1985.

White-Thomson, Stephen. Illustrations by Gerry Wood. *Elizabeth I and Tudor England.* New York: The Bookwright Press, 1985.

Zamoyska, Betka. *Queen Elizabeth I.* New York, St. Louis, San Francisco: McGraw-Hill Book Co., 1981.